Original title:
The Hollow Tree

Author: Aron Pilviste
ISBN HARDBACK: 978-9908-1-2605-0
ISBN PAPERBACK: 978-9908-1-2606-7
ISBN EBOOK: 978-9908-1-2607-4

Memories Entwined in Bark

In ancient trees where stories dwell,
The whispers of the past compel.
Roots gripping Earth, strong and deep,
In silence, memories safely sleep.

Bark wrapped tight, a living tome,
Every ring a tale of home.
Sun-kissed leaves in gentle sway,
Echoing the joys of day.

Cracks and scars tell of the storm,
Yet still they hold a gentle form.
Nature's touch, a tender grace,
In every inch, a timeless place.

When twilight comes, shadows play,
As coolness wraps the fading day.
Secrets held in every bend,
The forest speaks; it will not end.

Spirits of the Woodland

In twilight's glow, the spirits rise,
Among the trees where echoes lie.
A breeze that dances, soft and light,
Whispers secrets of the night.

Mossy blankets on the ground,
Where life and magic intertwine, unbound.
Silent watchers with watchful eyes,
In every rustle, the past replies.

Moonlit paths where shadows weave,
Nature holds what we believe.
A flicker here, a flutter there,
The woodland's breath fills the air.

Echoes of laughter long since faded,
In every glade, the lost are braided.
Through branches high, their voices soar,
Inviting all to seek for more.

Nestled in Nature's Arms

Cradled close by wooded grace,
Where wildflowers dare to embrace.
The scent of pine, the song of streams,
Nature's touch fulfills our dreams.

Honeyed rays of morning light,
Kiss the dew in soft delight.
A symphony of life unfolds,
The sweetest stories softly told.

Whispers of the gentle breeze,
Rustling leaves like secrets tease.
Sunset hues begin to glow,
Painting skies in fiery flow.

Nestled deep in roots below,
Life's pulse quickens, soft and slow.
Together, we find our way,
In nature's arms, forever stay.

The Sentinel of Seasons

Standing tall with ancient pride,
The sentinel waits with open side.
Witness to the passing years,
In laughter, joy, and silent tears.

Each season tells a different tale,
From winter's chill to summer's gale.
Vibrant change, a wondrous sight,
Underneath the stars' soft light.

Golden leaves in crisp, cool air,
Whisper stories of love and care.
In the silence of the night,
The sentinel holds the world tight.

Through tempest's wrath and sun's embrace,
A timeless guardian, steadfast space.
In every branch and every bark,
Life's continuity leaves its mark.

Murmurs of the Age-Old Canopy

Underneath the ancient trees,
Whispers stir in gentle breeze.
Leaves converse in nature's tongue,
Stories of the old days sung.

Branches sway with tales of yore,
Echoes of what came before.
Nostalgia swirls in dappled light,
Treasures hidden, out of sight.

Roots entwined in silent dance,
Nature's secrets, not by chance.
A world where time stands still,
Where magic bends to nature’s will.

Shadows play on forest floor,
Mysteries to be explored.
With every rustle, every sound,
Life's wonders are profound.

Amidst the boughs, we pause and breathe,
In this realm, we find reprieve.
The canopy, a timeless friend,
Murmurs softly without end.

Mysteries Wrapped in Leaf

In layers green, the stories hide,
Between each leaf, secrets bide.
Rustling softly, hints arise,
Mysteries dance beneath the skies.

Shadows cast by sun’s embrace,
Nature's wonders, every place.
Glimmers of a past untold,
Wrapped in leaves of green and gold.

Vivid hues beneath the sun,
Whispers of the earth’s soft run.
Each burst of color, a silent plea,
Nature's heart beats wild and free.

Through dewy mornings, soft and clear,
Ancient voices draw us near.
In every rustle, every sigh,
The wind carries time, drifting by.

So pause awhile and take a glance,
At every leaf, give truth a chance.
For in their form, a story we weave,
Mysteries forever up their sleeve.

Whispers in the Canopy

High above, the branches sway,
Whispers echo through the bay.
Leaves converse in hushed delight,
Secrets linger, out of sight.

In twilight's glow, the shadows blend,
Nature's magic seems to send.
A symphony of rustling leaves,
A gentle calm the forest weaves.

Birds in chorus, soft and sweet,
In harmony, their voices meet.
Each melody, a tale to share,
Whispers caught in evening air.

The canopy, a hidden world,
In every branch, a dream unfurled.
Listen closely, heed the call,
For whispers thrive among us all.

As stars peek through the leafy veil,
The night sings softly, tells a tale.
In the canopy, life will flow,
Whispers guiding where to go.

Peering into the Knothole

I peer through a knothole,
Curiosity's embrace,
The world beyond reveals,
Secrets time won't erase.

The whispers of the wind,
Speak tales of lost delight,
Of ages long forgotten,
And dreams that fade from sight.

A glimpse of verdant fields,
Where sunlight spills like gold,
Children laughing, running,
Their joys forever told.

A shadow passes by,
A fleeting, silent ghost,
Echoes of the past linger,
In memories we host.

Yet all remains a dream,
Just fragments of the dream,
Peering in, I wonder,
What life truly may seem.

Ceremony of the Oldest Oak

Beneath the ancient boughs,
Where history resides,
We gather in silence,
Where nature's heart abides.

The roots twist deep in earth,
A tapestry of time,
Each ring a story held,
In nature's verdant rhyme.

A sacred flame is lit,
To honor life and loss,
As whispers ride the breeze,
Our thoughts, a gentle toss.

We dance in shadow's glow,
Around the mighty trunk,
With each step, a promise,
In sunlight's warm spunk.

The ceremony unfolds,
As stars begin to gleam,
In unity we stand,
Embracing the same dream.

Pavilion of Soft Shadows

In gardens lush and green,
Where shadows softly play,
A pavilion of dreams waits,
For light to slip away.

The petals gently fall,
A carpet of hues bright,
While whispers in the breeze,
Carry secrets of the night.

With lanterns softly glowing,
Casting warmth in dark's embrace,
We gather round in silence,
Finding comfort in this space.

The laughter of the stars,
Weaves a melody so sweet,
Air thick with summertime,
Underneath our dancing feet.

In the pavilion's heart,
A stillness filled with grace,
Where every soul can linger,
And find their rightful place.

Tapestry of Life Above

Look up to woven skies,
A tapestry in flight,
Clouds like threads of silver,
Embroidering the night.

Sunset drapes the canvas,
In colors bold and bright,
Each hue a fleeting moment,
In the dance of fading light.

The stars begin to twinkle,
A quilt of dreams at play,
Guiding lost wanderers,
Throughout their starry way.

The moon, a gentle guardian,
Watches over each soul,
Binding all together,
In the sky's eternal scroll.

In this tapestry of life,
We find our hearts entwined,
A connection to the heavens,
In the beauty we can find.

Mystery in the Green Twilight

In the whispering woods so deep,
Shadows dance while the night creeps.
Leaves rustle with secrets untold,
Embracing wonders, both timid and bold.

Moonlight spills through branches twined,
Casting dreams that softly bind.
Mysteries linger, thick as smoke,
As ancient tales in silence choke.

Crickets sing their evening song,
Echoes of dusk where we belong.
Stars shimmer in a velvet sky,
Calling us to wander and fly.

Footsteps tread on paths unknown,
In the twilight's grasp, we are shown.
Answers hide where shadows loom,
Awakening hearts from their gloom.

Together we’ll seek the hidden glade,
Where the light of dawn won't fade.
In the mystery, we find our way,
In the green twilight, come what may.

Fragments of Lost Journeys

In the ash of forgotten maps,
Whispers linger, time overlaps.
Stories woven in threads of gold,
Echoes of hearts that once were bold.

Footprints fade on paths of sand,
Each step a whisper, a guiding hand.
Memories twirl like leaves in flight,
Fleeting glimpses of former light.

Dreams shattered on craggy shores,
Castaway thoughts by turbulent roars.
Fragments glimmer, pieces align,
Remnants of journeys once divine.

Tales of wonder laced with pain,
Touch the heart, like a gentle rain.
Lost and found, we chase the dawn,
In every ending, a new song drawn.

Through valleys deep and mountains high,
We seek the stars in the endless sky.
Each fragment a promise to embrace,
In every journey, we find our place.

Starlit Vows Among the Branches

Underneath the shimmering night,
We share our dreams in soft moonlight.
Branches weave like fingers entwined,
A promise whispered, love defined.

Stars twinkle in the midnight hue,
Witness to every vow so true.
The world silent, hearts laid bare,
In this moment, nothing can compare.

Leaves murmur secrets, sweet and low,
As shadows dance, the soft wind blows.
Every glance speaks, every sigh,
Under the heavens, you and I.

Time stands still, the night unfolds,
In your eyes, a universe holds.
Starlit vows, a sacred song,
Together still, where we belong.

Among the branches, love will thrive,
In this embrace, we come alive.
Forever bound by destiny's thread,
Under the stars, our hearts are led.

A Tangle of Forgotten Dreams

In the attic, dust dances light,
Old photographs whisper at night.
A tangle of memories waits in the gloom,
Longing to break free, to bloom.

Each corner holds a shadowed sigh,
Fragments of laughter, a fleeting high.
Dreams once vibrant now covered in dust,
Awaiting the moment when we will trust.

Threads of time weave tales around,
In every silence, echoes are found.
Forgotten faces, stories untold,
In the maze of the past, we feel bold.

Rekindling visions lost in the race,
Finding ourselves in the cherished space.
Every dream a path to retrace,
In the tangle, we embrace.

Through the layers, we sift and seek,
In each reveal, our spirits speak.
From the shadows, the bright emerge,
A tapestry of life, we urge.

Heartwood Hush

In the stillness of the trees,
Whispers weave through gentle breeze.
Branches cradle dreams untold,
Heartwood secrets, timeless, bold.

Rustling leaves in twilight's gleam,
Carry echoes of a dream.
Nature's pulse, a tender sigh,
Beneath the vast and starry sky.

Mossy carpets softly cling,
Lulling nature's quiet spring.
Luminous fireflies take flight,
Guiding hearts through velvet night.

Silhouettes of roots entwined,
In this haven, peace we find.
Every heartbeat, every hush,
Holds the world in sacred trust.

So let us linger, breathe, and pause,
In this hush, we find our cause.
With each blink, the dusk unfolds,
Heartwood whispers, soft and bold.

Refuge of Forgotten Tales

Within the shadows, stories glow,
Ancient whispers, soft and slow.
Pages turning, time stands still,
Echoes of a distant thrill.

Tattered books and faded ink,
Hold the past as we now think.
Every tale a gentle call,
In the refuge, we lose all.

Whirlwinds of the lost embrace,
Bring to life a fleeting grace.
Voices linger, never fade,
In the nook where dreams are made.

Candles flicker, shadows sway,
Guiding spirits on their way.
Each forgotten tale takes flight,
In the tapestry of night.

A haven wrapped in mystery,
Time's embrace, a symphony.
In this refuge, hearts ignite,
Forgotten tales bloom in light.

Moonlit Sanctuary

In a haven bathed in white,
Moonlit shadows dance with light.
Every whisper of the night,
Holds a promise, soft and bright.

Silver beams on tranquil streams,
Guide the weary into dreams.
Nature's lullaby unfolds,
As the universe beholds.

Crickets serenade the dark,
With their soft and gentle spark.
Underneath the stellar dome,
All the wandering souls find home.

Cypress candles flicker low,
Casting warmth in twilight's flow.
In this sanctuary divine,
Hearts entwine, and souls align.

As the night begins to fade,
Memories and dreams are made.
Moonlit paths will guide the way,
Until the break of dawning day.

Shade of the Silent Grove

In the grove where silence lies,
Whispers drift beneath the skies.
Leaves embrace the softest sound,
In this sanctuary profound.

Petals scatter in the breeze,
Nature plays her melodies.
Ancient roots, a tale of grace,
Finding warmth in nature's space.

Sunlight dapples through the leaves,
Casting shadows, peace achieves.
Moments linger, gently swayed,
In the shade, our worries fade.

Butterflies on lazy wings,
Float through life, embrace what sings.
Underneath the silent trees,
Nature holds us, soft as fleece.

Let us breathe the tranquil air,
In the grove, we shed our care.
As the sun begins to rise,
Peaceful hearts find sweet reprise.

Spirit of the Dappled Light

In glades where whispers play,
The sunbeams dance and sway.
They waltz on emerald leaves,
A symphony that weaves.

A shimmer bright and bold,
Stories of the forest told.
Soft shadows come alive,
In this magic they thrive.

Within the twilight's embrace,
Every corner finds its space.
Mysteries unfold with grace,
Nature’s gentle, sacred place.

Through branches intertwined,
The spirit’s essence shines.
In each flicker of the sun,
The dance of life’s begun.

Beneath a sky so vast,
The fleeting moments cast.
In dappled light we find,
The heart of earth aligned.

Legacy of the Lost Canopy

In the silence of the trees,
Echoes of a time that flees.
Where roots of yore still cling,
To forgotten tales they bring.

Leaves fall like whispered sighs,
Underneath the azure skies.
Faded blossoms speak of dreams,
Hold close the past, it gleams.

Once vibrant, now a hush,
Nature's breath, a gentle rush.
Memories in every grain,
A soft touch of joy and pain.

The whispers of the night,
Reveal remnants of their flight.
Guardians of what once stood tall,
Call for us to heed their call.

In shadows deep and wide,
Legacies we cannot hide.
The canopies may fade away,
Yet their spirits still will stay.

Beneath the Enchanted Skin

Beneath the bark, a heartbeat lies,
Secrets hidden from our eyes.
Vibrations soft, like tender sighs,
In nature's arms, where magic flies.

The earth, a tapestry of dreams,
Whispers of life in flowing streams.
Each cell, a testament to grace,
A dance, a song, a sacred place.

In every petal, story wakes,
A world of wonder, for our sake.
The dew drops hold the morning light,
As shadows play, and day turns bright.

With every breeze, the tales unfold,
Memories of the young and old.
Connect the dots with gentle hands,
Embrace the magic in the lands.

Beneath the skin of all we see,
Lies an enchantment, wild and free.
In unity, we find our kin,
Listen closely, let life begin.

Guardian of Nature’s Secrets

In twilight's hue, a figure stands,
With watchful eyes and gentle hands.
The guardian keeps the forest's lore,
Protecting treasures evermore.

Through hushed whispers of the night,
A solemn promise takes its flight.
To shield the wild, both fierce and meek,
Ensuring that the earth can speak.

In tangled vines and velvet moss,
Ancient wisdom, never lost.
The spirit of the trees and streams,
Infused with love, fulfills our dreams.

With every rustling leaf and sigh,
Nature breathes, and soars to the sky.
The guardian knows each sacred fold,
Within the warmth, the tales unfold.

Enshrined in balance, they remain,
The herald of the sweet refrain.
In harmony, they fight and strive,
For in their care, we all shall thrive.

Echoes in the Canopy

Leaves rustle softly, a gentle sigh,
Birds call to one another, soaring high.
Sunlight filters through a green embrace,
Nature's symphony finds its place.

Branches sway, a dance of calm,
Moments captured, like an ancient psalm.
Whispers in the wind, secrets told,
Within the trees, mysteries unfold.

Shadows shift beneath the boughs,
Time stands still, and silence vows.
Every rustling leaf has a tale to share,
In the canopy's cradle, we breathe the air.

Echoes linger in the quiet night,
Stars peek through, a canvas of light.
Nature cradles dreams in her hand,
Guiding us gently, through this enchanted land.

Underneath the vast, twinkling sky,
We find ourselves, learning to fly.
Together we wander, hearts set free,
In the echoes of the canopy, we shall be.

Secrets of the Ancient Boughs

Boughs twisted, with stories to tell,
Guardians of time, in their shadows dwell.
Worn by the passage of endless years,
In their embrace, we shed our fears.

Gnarled roots weave beneath the earth,
Each one cradles a secret's birth.
Whispers of ages, soft and low,
Carried by wind, where no one goes.

Sunlight bathes the weathered bark,
Each ring a memory, a silent mark.
Moss cloaked whispers, ancient and wise,
In the boughs' silence, the truth lies.

Foliage trembles as dusk draws near,
The night reveals what the day won't clear.
In shadows deep, where spirits roam,
The ancient tale finds its home.

With every breeze, a heartbeat sighs,
In the boughs' cradle, our spirit flies.
Secrets held tight in nature's thrall,
In whispers of boughs, we hear it all.

Whispering Roots

Roots entwined beneath the ground,
Silent stories waiting to be found.
Tangled pathways stretch and weave,
In their depth, we dare believe.

Softly they murmur, a gentle song,
Tales of the earth, where we belong.
Feel their heartbeat, a rhythmic flow,
In the dark, life starts to grow.

Nurtured by rain and kissed by light,
Roots cradle dreams hidden from sight.
Every inch tells of love and strife,
Whispers echo the dance of life.

As the seasons change, they stretch and sigh,
Reaching for stars in the endless sky.
Boundless in spirit, they rise and fall,
In whispering roots, we hear nature's call.

Together we journey, hand in hand,
In the heart of the earth, we make our stand.
With wisdom grounded, we find our truth,
The secrets of roots, a fountain of youth.

A Sanctuary of Shadows

In twilight's glow, shadows start to blend,
Whispers linger where the pathways bend.
Soft twilight veil, a tender touch,
In this sanctuary, we feel so much.

Leaves dance lightly, casting their spell,
Every crevice where secrets dwell.
Darkness cradles the fading light,
A gentle hush encases the night.

Beneath the branches, shadows rise,
Unraveling dreams beneath the skies.
In the stillness, heartbeats twine,
A sanctuary where souls align.

Time slows down as the stars appear,
In this embrace, there's nothing to fear.
Echoes of laughter fill the air,
Within the shadows, love laid bare.

As moonlight spills on the forest floor,
We trace the contours of hidden lore.
In twilight's haven, we find our peace,
A sanctuary of shadows, where wonders cease.

Reverent Resilience

In darkest nights, we stand so tall,
Finding strength within the fall.
With quiet grace, we mend our seams,
Awakening the boldest dreams.

Through storms that rage, we hold our ground,
In whispers soft, our hopes are found.
Each bruise a mark, a tale to tell,
Of standing firm, of breaking well.

With every trial, our spirits soar,
Rooted deep, we seek for more.
In shadows cast, we find the light,
Together strong, we face the fight.

Through valleys low and peaks so high,
We lift our gaze, we touch the sky.
A tapestry of scars we wear,
A legacy of love and care.

In hearts united, we will rise,
Resilience reigns, and fear defies.
With every heartbeat, hope persists,
A promise held in morning mist.

The Heart of the Forest

Among the trees, the whispers call,
Nature's breath, a gentle thrall.
Leaves dance lightly, shadows play,
In the forest, night meets day.

Roots entwined beneath the earth,
Cradle stories of our birth.
Beneath the boughs, the silence sings,
Life's embrace, the joy it brings.

Mossy carpets line the path,
Flickers of light, the sun's sweet wrath.
Every breeze, a song of grace,
In this wild, enchanted space.

Creatures scurry, branches sway,
Nature's heart beats night and day.
In emerald depths, we find our way,
To the heartbeat of the stay.

With every step, we tread so light,
In the forest, shadows bite.
Yet hope thrives where silence reigns,
The heart of the woods, our souls' remains.

Memory’s Arbor

In twilight’s glow, the past unfolds,
Whispers of stories, softly told.
Beneath the boughs of time's embrace,
We gather fragments, find our place.

A smile preserved, a touch so dear,
In memory's grip, we hold them near.
Each moment lives within our hearts,
A tapestry where love imparts.

The shadows lengthen, seasons change,
Yet memories remain, un-strange.
In every tear, a lesson learned,
In every laugh, the heart has burned.

Beneath the trees of memory's grove,
We seek the warmth of those we love.
Each leaf a tale, each branch a dream,
Together woven, a gentle stream.

Through winding paths of yesteryears,
We walk with grace, embracing fears.
For in the garden of our mind,
The sweetest blooms are often kind.

The Shaded Haven

Beneath the canopy, we find our peace,
A sanctuary where worries cease.
Dappled sunlight on the forest floor,
In this haven, we long for more.

The rustling leaves, a soothing song,
In this refuge, we belong.
Gentle breezes, whispers low,
In shaded corners, calm will grow.

Nature's arms embrace our souls,
Filling up our sacred goals.
With every breath, the spirit lifts,
In this haven, the heart gifts.

Moments linger, tender and sweet,
In the stillness, our hearts meet.
Through tangled branches, joy cascades,
In this shaded world, love parades.

As twilight falls, the stars appear,
In our haven, night draws near.
With hopes renewed under starry skies,
In nature’s peace, our spirit flies.

Life in the Knotted Embrace

In shadows deep where secrets lie,
Roots entwined, they reach the sky.
Whispers echo in the night,
Holding dreams in fading light.

Branches cradle the hopes we cling,
In every leaf, the memories sing.
Love and loss in tangled vine,
A dance of fate, forever entwined.

Through storms that break, we'll find our way,
Knot by knot, we brave the fray.
Hands held tight, together we stand,
In this embrace, forever planned.

Peace grows wild in the knotted maze,
A symphony of life's praise.
Through trials faced, we rise above,
In the heart of the knotted love.

In twilight's glow, the journey starts,
Each twist and turn connects hearts.
From roots below to skies above,
Life pulses forth in knotted love.

Stories Woven in Twigs

Beneath the trees where shadows play,
Nature's canvas holds sway.
Twigs and whispers tell the tales,
Of distant lands and gales.

Each knot holds secrets, old and wise,
In their embrace, the past lies.
Gentle breezes dance along,
Carrying the forest’s song.

Branches weave a tapestry bright,
Under the soft, starlit night.
Gathered round in twilight's veil,
Stories shared like a sailor's tale.

Every heart a story binds,
In the rustle, wisdom finds.
Through time's flow, we weave and spin,
Life’s adventures tucked within.

In the quiet, tales unfold,
Woven whispers, brave and bold.
Nature's art is ever clear,
In the twigs, our stories steer.

Breath of the Forest

In emerald depths where silence dwells,
The forest breathes and softly tells.
Pure air thick with ancient lore,
Nature's rhythm, a steady score.

Leaves converse in rustling tones,
Echoes of life in nature's bones.
Each sigh carries a timeless truth,
The wisdom born from sun and youth.

Moss-clad trails, a path to grace,
Whispers of time in every place.
Through canopy, the sunlight streams,
Waking the world from shadowed dreams.

In twilight’s hush, the forest glows,
Breathing life and nurturing flows.
With every gust, each branch does sway,
In the breath of the forest, we play.

Harmony thrives in the woodlands’ heart,
In each heartbeat, a work of art.
Beneath the sky, so vast and pure,
Breath of the forest, forever sure.

The Meeting of Spirits

In twilight’s glow where shadows blend,
Two spirits dance, their paths transcend.
Among the trees, in whispers sweet,
Their ancient souls, in silence meet.

A flicker of light, a gentle sigh,
Among the stars, they rise and fly.
Bound by fate, through time they roam,
In the night, they find their home.

Beneath the moon, the air does hum,
A sacred place where dreams are spun.
With every breath, the stories weave,
In the meeting, they truly believe.

Hands of the past, future’s embrace,
In the dance, they find their place.
Spirits join in harmony’s thread,
In the still of night, fears are shed.

Through echoes soft, their voices call,
In the communion, they stand tall.
Two spirits bound in timeless grace,
In the meeting, they find their space.

Secrets in the Shade

In the grove where whispers dwell,
Secrets weave a silent spell.
Under branches, shadows creep,
Nature's promises we keep.

Echoes of the past resound,
In the quiet, truth is found.
Gentle breezes carry dreams,
Softly flowing, like the streams.

Mossy stones and tangled roots,
Hidden tales, forgotten truths.
In the shade, the heart will sway,
Sharing what the light won't say.

Flickering lights through leaves above,
Nature speaks of life and love.
In each rustle, softly bared,
Whispers of the lives once shared.

Here in shadows, time stands still,
Every secret, every thrill.
Dancing patterns, dusk and dawn,
In the shade, the world feels drawn.

The Gathering of the Autumn Leaves

Orange whispers fill the air,
As the leaves begin to share.
Swaying gently, soft and free,
Gathering tales from each tree.

Crisp and cracking underfoot,
Nature's carpet, brightly put.
Breezes sing a playful tune,
While the sun bows to the moon.

Cheerful colors swirl and dance,
In their fleeting, bold romance.
Every leaf a story told,
In the autumn's glowing gold.

Fleeting moments, time's embrace,
Nature's beauty, a warm trace.
Gathered round in twilight's glow,
Memories of summer's flow.

In this fleeting, golden haze,
Life unfolds in autumn's phase.
Each leaf falling, free and brave,
Marks the path that echoes save.

Remnants of Light and Shadow

Sunlight dances on the walls,
Casting shadows, nature calls.
In the twilight, secrets bloom,
Living here within the gloom.

Faint reflections softly play,
In the corners, night and day.
Traces of the heart we hold,
Stories shared, both brave and bold.

Lingers light, a fleeting kiss,
In the shadows, find your bliss.
Every flicker tells a tale,
In this harmony, we sail.

Echoed dreams, they rise and fall,
In the silence, hear the call.
Remnants wrapped in twilight's thread,
Whisper softly, hearts are fed.

With each shadow, light remains,
In the dance of wins and gains.
Holding onto what we see,
In this balance, we are free.

Where Memories Root

Deep in soil, where whispers dwell,
Memories bloom, cast their spell.
From the past, a tender shoot,
In the garden, where roots suit.

Every petal tells a phrase,
In the sunlight's golden gaze.
Nurtured by the hope we share,
In this garden, love laid bare.

Time will weave its gentle thread,
Through the living, through the dead.
Every heartbeat, every sigh,
Lingers softly, drifting by.

Here the laughter, here the tears,
Echo softly through the years.
In this space, our futures grow,
Where the heart and spirit flow.

Lost in reverie, we find,
Tales of love, forever bind.
In the roots, our stories dwell,
In this garden, all is well.

Nature's Hidden Embrace

In the forest deep and wide,
Where secrets of the earth abide.
Whispers of the wind do call,
Inviting us to heed their thrall.

Sunlight dances on the streams,
Cradling all forgotten dreams.
A symphony of rustling leaves,
Nature weaves what the heart believes.

Mountains rise with silent pride,
Guardians where the spirits hide.
Each petal soft, a tender sigh,
In blooms that reach toward the sky.

Streams meander, soft and slow,
Through vale and glen where wildflowers grow.
Each corner holds a hidden grace,
In nature’s warm and wild embrace.

As twilight falls and stars ignite,
The moon unveils its silver light.
We find our peace in nature's heart,
Forever linked, we'll never part.

The Emissary of the Wild

A spirited fox darts through tall grass,
With keen eyes watching as moments pass.
The echoes of dusk call out her name,
In nature’s realm, she's free and untamed.

With whispers of secrets under moon's gaze,
She leads explorers through twilight's haze.
Every rustle a tale of survival,
An emblem of nature’s raw revival.

As night descends, her journey unfolds,
Through ancient woods and tales untold.
Each pawprint carved into the earth,
A reminder of wildness, a sacred birth.

In shadows deep, where the creatures play,
She beckons wanderers to find their way.
A bridge between worlds, both fierce and mild,
The wild runs free, with her, a wild child.

In the heart of the forest, her spirit soars,
A guide through the dreams that nature restores.
With every heartbeat, she flows like air,
The emissary of the wild, always there.

Shadows Cast on Ancient Life

Beneath the boughs of timeless trees,
Whispering tales carried by the breeze.
Echoes of creatures that once roamed here,
Their spirits linger, forever near.

In quiet glades where shadows dance,
Life weaves a tapestry, a voiceless romance.
Fossils and stones tell stories profound,
Of ages past, where wonders abound.

Every rustling leaf, a memory stirred,
The tales of the past in silence heard.
With sunlight filtering through the green,
A canvas painted with the unseen.

Across the valley, the legends sigh,
In the twilight's glow as the day waves goodbye.
The silhouette of wisdom speaks,
In nature's heart, the ancient seeks.

Timeless rhythms, a cycle of grace,
In shadows cast, we find our place.
Among the whispers of ancient life,
We tread softly, away from strife.

Luminescence in the Darkness

As shadows stretch in the fading light,
The stars awaken, embracing the night.
Glowing softly with stories to tell,
Each twinkling point, a wish cast well.

In the depths of night, fireflies gleam,
Dancing like hopes within a dream.
They flicker and shimmer, a radiant choir,
Illuminating paths with gentle fire.

The moonlit glow kisses the trees,
Whispering secrets carried by the breeze.
A luminous canvas in deep navy skies,
Where shadows and light harmoniously rise.

Above the world, calm and serene,
Night wraps the earth in a silken sheen.
A refuge for hearts seeking peace,
In darkness, the soul finds release.

As the dawn breaks, the stars fade away,
But the glow lingers, a bright ballet.
In the heart of night, we find our way,
In the luminescence, come what may.

The Enigma of Every Ring

In circles drawn on ancient wood,
A story whispered, understood.
Each layer tells a tale of time,
In silences, they softly chime.

A golden band, a promise kept,
In shadows deep, where memories slept.
The weight of trust, it softly clings,
The magic held within the rings.

From finger to finger, love's embrace,
Glimmers softly, a sacred space.
Within its round, a world confined,
A mystery shaped by hearts entwined.

With every twist, a hope takes flight,
Reflecting dreams in soft moonlight.
Each turn reveals what fate can bring,
The enigma found in every ring.

Guardian of Nature's Secrets

In the canopy where shadows play,
A guardian watches through the day.
With every leaf that rustles low,
Whispers of wisdom gently flow.

Beneath the roots, the secrets lie,
In every brook, in every sigh.
Listen closely, the heart will know,
The tales of ages that ebb and flow.

The winds carry stories, old and wise,
Of skies once bright, of darkened skies.
This nature's keeper, silent and grand,
Holds the threads of a complex strand.

For time won’t erase its gentle reign,
Life’s rhythms pulse through joy and pain.
In the stillness, we learn to see,
The harmony in each mystery.

Tales Twined with Vines

In gardens lush with green embrace,
Old stories twist, find their place.
Vines entwined in a lover's dance,
Whisper of fate, a second chance.

With every tendril, secrets weave,
A tapestry that hopes to cleave.
Beneath the trellis, shadows creep,
Guarding promise, nearly asleep.

Through sunlit days and starry nights,
The dance of life, the heart ignites.
In nature's arms, we share our dreams,
And realize how fleeting it seems.

In the rustling leaves, a song unfolds,
Tales of love, of lost and bold.
With every bud, new stories bloom,
Eternally caught in that verdant room.

Echoed Laughter and Forgotten Tears

In empty rooms where memories linger,
Whispers of joy slip through our fingers.
Laughter echoes off the walls,
Resonating through the silent halls.

Each corner holds a secret smile,
A trace of moments, a fleeting trial.
Yet shadows fall where sorrows tread,
Forgotten tears that softly bled.

Through winding paths of time we weave,
What once was bright, we learn to grieve.
But in the echoes, life still sings,
A harmony of both the stings.

So let us cherish every sound,
In laughter's light, the lost are found.
Together woven, joy and grief,
In every heartbeat, we find relief.

The Secret Life of Trees

In the quiet of the wood,
Where secrets softly tread,
Roots are tangled pathways,
Underneath the earth's bed.

Leaves whisper ancient tales,
In the gentle summer breeze,
Bark bears the scars of time,
Holding memories with ease.

Birds find shelter high above,
Singing songs of joy and peace,
While mushrooms softly bloom below,
Life's dance will never cease.

Branches stretch towards the sky,
A shelter for feathered friends,
In their shade, the world slows down,
Where nature's magic blends.

Each tree a living story,
Rooted deep, reaching wide,
Guardians of the forest,
In them, the secrets hide.

Guardians of the Green

Tall they stand, the guardians,
Cloaked in emerald hues,
Watching over all that moves,
In their watchful views.

Branches cradle nests in arms,
Where woodland creatures play,
Keeping watch through storm and calm,
Through night and brightening day.

Their trunks hold stories old,
Of storms and sunny skies,
Each ring reveals a year,
A memory that never dies.

Roots delve deep in silence,
Binding life to ground,
In this tranquil balance,
Where harmony is found.

Guardians of the green expanse,
They teach us how to grow,
In their shade, we find a chance,
To learn what they know.

Hidden Whispers of the Forest

In the forest, whispers soft,
Swaying leaves begin to talk,
Mossy carpets cushion steps,
Underneath the winding walk.

Sunlight dapples through the trees,
Creating patterns on the ground,
Nature’s art is vibrant here,
In every shadow, magic found.

Each twig snaps with a secret,
As critters scurry by,
Life unfolds in softest tones,
Beneath the vast blue sky.

Streams murmur ancient stories,
As stones listen, still and wise,
Every drop a memory,
Of rains and splendid skies.

Hidden whispers of the woods,
Call to those who dare to hear,
In the silence of the trees,
Nature's voice becomes quite clear.

Where Stories Take Root

Deep beneath the soil,
Where ancient roots entwine,
Stories lie in waiting,
In the darkness, they define.

Fingers of the trees reach out,
Grasping what is left behind,
In their embrace, the past awaits,
A future intertwined.

Each ring a tale, each leaf a song,
Of seasons spent and years,
Echoes of the life above,
Translating joys and fears.

Gentle breezes carry sounds,
Of laughter and of cries,
In the forest, life abounds,
Underneath vast, open skies.

Where stories softly take root,
In the heart of every glen,
Nature pens its volumes,
In the silence, time begins.

Cracked Shells and Whispers

In twilight's glow, the whispers sway,
Cracked shells lie where dreams decay.
The secrets held in fragile forms,
Echo softly, as night transforms.

Barefoot steps on sandy shores,
Each sound carries ancient roars.
A dance of shadows, light, and sound,
In broken whispers, truth is found.

The tides unravel tales untold,
In every crevice, life unfolds.
Silken threads of stars cascade,
Amongst the shells, memories fade.

What once was whole is now a shard,
Yet beauty lingers, never marred.
The ocean hums its lullaby,
As cracked shells keep the secrets nigh.

With every whisper, a lesson learned,
Through cracked shells, the fire burned.
Fragmented lives in shades of gold,
In breaking, stories still unfold.

Refuge of the Fleeting Breeze

In the meadow where the flowers sway,
The breeze whispers secrets of the day.
Dancing lightly through the trees,
A gentle touch, a soft reprieve.

Clouds drift slowly, shadows play,
An ethereal moment slips away.
Petals flutter with a sigh,
In the refuge where dreams can lie.

As sunlight weaves through branches tall,
The breeze carries nature's call.
Each whisper tells of love and loss,
In fleeting moments, we find gloss.

A spark of life in every sigh,
The breeze, a friend that drifts on high.
Collecting hopes, like fallen leaves,
In its embrace, the heart believes.

With every gust, a promise made,
Guiding spirits through the glade.
The world is vast, yet close we feel,
In a fleeting breeze, love is real.

Harbinger of Endless Seasons

The trees, they bend with tales untold,
In whispers of the winds, so bold.
Seasons pass, like fleeting dreams,
Transforming all with silent schemes.

Frost bites deep as shadows grow,
Yet every heart begins to glow.
A promise hidden in the cold,
A harbinger of warmth unfolds.

Spring awakens with colors bright,
Painted scenes in morning light.
Each bloom a wish upon the breeze,
A melody that aims to please.

Summer burns with golden rays,
A tapestry of sunlit days.
As laughter echoes through the air,
Time stands still, with naught a care.

Autumn whispers with a sigh,
Leaves dance downward in the sky.
A final bow before the night,
Echoes of life, in fading light.

The Gathering of Silent Witnesses

Underneath the silver moon,
The stars begin their glowing tune.
Silent watchers gather near,
Observing joys, and every fear.

Each flicker holds a story brief,
In whispered tales of joy and grief.
A gathering in celestial embrace,
Time and space, they interlace.

Mountains high, with shadows cast,
Bear witness to the present, past.
Ancient trees stand strong and tall,
Silent echoes of nature's call.

In the stillness, secrets dwell,
In every heartbeat, tales to tell.
Fragrant breezes softly sweep,
Bringing forth the dreams we keep.

In twilight's cloak, they hold our gaze,
The silent witnesses through the haze.
With every breath, they weave our fate,
In cosmic dance, the heart awaits.

Hiding in the Underbrush

Among the leaves, I lie in wait,
A world alive at nature's gate.
Small creatures stir, the shadows play,
In quietude, I lose the day.

The rustling grass, a hush descends,
As sunlight fades and twilight blends.
Each breath a story, softly heard,
In whispered tones, reply a bird.

The scent of earth, the dampened pine,
Where dreams of freedom intertwine.
I watch the dance of life unfold,
In underbrush, my heart takes hold.

Each moment paused, in still embrace,
A fleeting glimpse of nature's grace.
I hold the secrets, thick and lush,
In this cocoon, a gentle hush.

As day gives way to velvet night,
I find my peace in fading light.
Beneath the stars, my spirit soars,
In hiding, I am evermore.

Reverie of the Dappled Sun

Through branches high, the sunlight streams,
Awakening the hidden dreams.
On painted paths of gold and green,
A dance of shadows, soft and keen.

Upon the ground, the dappled glow,
In fleeting moments, time does flow.
I wander where the laughter plays,
And nature sings, in warm embrace.

The breeze, it whispers secrets new,
As flowers nod with morning dew.
A tapestry of light and hue,
In reverie of sweet, sunlit view.

As every leaf begins to sway,
The heart finds joy in fleeting day.
In gentle warmth, I lose my cares,
Among the sunbeams, laughter flares.

Each heartbeat pulses with the light,
In dappled realms, my soul takes flight.
Forever caught in golden spun,
I dwell within this dappled sun.

A Portal to the Past

In shadows deep, a door appears,
A portal waits, it calls my fears.
Through mist and time, I take a glance,
Where echoes of lost moments dance.

The whispers soft of days gone by,
A fleeting touch, a wonder why.
With every step, I see the road,
Where memories softly erode.

Old photographs, a faded hue,
With laughter shared, and friendships true.
In fragments bright, the past returns,
A flickering flame, the heart still burns.

With every breath, a story wakes,
In misty trails, the present quakes.
The weight of time, a gentle guide,
To where my heart and dreams abide.

Through this portal, I should not dwell,
But linger here, I know too well.
In shadows deep, I feel the cast,
In every thought, a portal vast.

Where Whispers Find Refuge

In quiet nooks, the whispers play,
Where secrets tread on soft ballet.
Beneath the boughs, in silence steeped,
The stories shared, a promise kept.

The gentle hum of nature's song,
As shadows stretch, they wander long.
In murmured tones, the leaves respond,
To echoes of the heart’s true bond.

With every breeze, a sigh released,
In stillness found, a moment feast.
Where hope and fear in silence blend,
In whispered dreams, we always mend.

The world outside may rush and race,
Yet here, we find our sacred space.
Where whispers linger, soft and sweet,
In refuge found, our hearts compete.

As twilight falls, we gather near,
In whispered tales, we shed our fear.
A sanctuary where we trust,
In whispered bonds, our love is just.

Refuge for the Wandering Heart

In shadows deep, a whisper calls,
A place where silence gently falls.
The road is long, the night is dark,
Yet here I'll find a guiding spark.

Beneath the stars, my spirit soars,
Through open skies and ancient shores.
The echoes of my fears now cease,
And in this stillness, I find peace.

With every step, I shed my doubt,
A quiet strength I can't live without.
Around me blooms a tender grace,
In solitude, I find my place.

The heart that wanders seeks to know,
The stories written in the glow.
I gather dreams like autumn leaves,
In this refuge, my soul believes.

So let the world spin wild and free,
In this small space, I'll always be.
For here within, love softly tarts,
To dwell forever, wandering hearts.

Cracks in the Bark

On ancient trees, the stories lie,
Carved by time, as seasons sigh.
Each crack a tale, a moment's past,
In nature’s grip, our shadows cast.

Through whispered winds, the branches bend,
A dance with light that will not end.
Beneath the bark, a heartbeat waits,
In every knot, a life narrates.

The forest breathes with secrets old,
And secrets new are slowly told.
A cerulean sky, profound and wide,
Where lost travelers often hide.

Underneath, the roots entwine,
As nature’s hand draws forth the line.
In cracks of bark, we find our way,
Through shadowed night, to brightening day.

Let every flaw and every mark,
Be seen as strength and lighten dark.
For even in the weathered wood,
The beauty lies where cracks once stood.

Timeless Guardian of Solitude

In twilight's glow, the stillness reigns,
A whisper soft, breaks inner chains.
The lonely path, it winds away,
Yet here, I choose to gently stay.

The oak, a watcher, vast and wise,
Holds secrets close beneath the skies.
In its embrace, my worries melt,
A tranquil space where hope is felt.

Time drips slow like honey sweet,
In solitude, my heart's retreat.
The ticking clock slows down its pace,
In this stillness, I find my place.

Around me echoes nature's song,
Each note a balm for what feels wrong.
The whispers of the past unfold,
As tales of love and loss retold.

With every breath, I sense the dawn,
The guard of time, a binding bond.
In quietude, the world anew,
A guardian of me and of you.

The Shelter of Lost Souls

In corners dark, where shadows creep,
The shelter stands, a home to keep.
For broken hearts and weary minds,
A solace found, true love entwined.

Within these walls, the stories blend,
Of laughter lost and time to spend.
With every tear, a lesson learned,
In the soft glow, the candle burned.

The whispers float like distant dreams,
Awakening hope, or so it seems.
In every heart, a tale resides,
Of journeys long and secret tides.

As night descends, the lanterns glow,
A beacon bright for those who roam.
No longer lost, the souls now find,
The tender light that once was blind.

So let the past forever fade,
In the shelter, love won't trade.
For every soul that finds its way,
In unity, we choose to stay.

Secrets of the Ancient Wood

Whispers dance upon the breeze,
Ancient trees hold tales with ease.
Roots entwined in mystery,
Secrets lie beneath the tree.

Moonlight filters through the leaves,
Ghostly shadows softly weave.
In twilight's calm, the spirits sigh,
Guardians of the night sky high.

Time stands still in sacred hush,
Rustling leaves, a gentle rush.
Hidden paths and trails unfold,
Stories waiting to be told.

Echoes linger in the glade,
Memories of the forest made.
In each crack and whisper soft,
Lies the essence of the loft.

Footsteps trace the ancient ground,
Where lost souls may still be found.
In the heart of wood so deep,
The ancient trees in silence keep.

Echoes of a Forgotten Grove

In shadows thick, the whispers dwell,
A grove where age-old stories swell.
Faded echoes linger near,
Carrying tales for those who hear.

Mossy stones and twisted vines,
Mark the place where magic shines.
Beneath the boughs, the air is sweet,
In this realm where past and present meet.

Ghostly figures softly roam,
In this lush and leafy dome.
With every rustle, secrets rise,
Hidden truths where nature lies.

The sky above in colors sway,
Painting night to chase the day.
Time slips gently, like a stream,
Bringing forth a fading dream.

Leaves murmur with a soft embrace,
As memories find their rightful place.
Echoes linger, softly call,
In the sacred grove, we feel it all.

Shadows Among the Boughs

Beneath the boughs where shadows play,
Quiet moments stretch and sway.
Dappled light through branches weaves,
Casting patterns on soft leaves.

A rustle speaks of hidden things,
In the wood, where nature sings.
Each step reveals a world unknown,
In the heart of the forest grown.

The gentle hush of evening's breath,
Echos softly of life and death.
In twilight's glow, the spirits dance,
In the shadows, they take their chance.

Secrets held within the bark,
Await the wanderer's gentle mark.
With whispers there to guide the way,
Through the night and into day.

Underneath the ancient oak,
Mysteries in silence spoke.
In shadows deep, the stories blend,
Among the boughs, the tales transcend.

Heart of the Enchanted Trunk

In the heart of the trunk so wide,
Mysteries of nature abide.
With roots that drink from ancient streams,
And branches that cradle dreams.

Cocooned in bark, a realm of grace,
Where time slips by without a trace.
Each knot and gnarled twist reveals,
Life's tapestry of whispered deals.

Winds of change gently blow,
Through the leaves, secrets flow.
A tapestry of sun and rain,
In every ring, a joy or pain.

Innocent eyes gaze upon,
The stories woven till the dawn.
In nature’s heart, we find our place,
Entranced by this enchanted space.

So linger long, let shadows meld,
In the trunk where dreams are held.
For in this wood, you shall discern,
The magic waits for you to learn.

The Echoing Bough

Beneath the ancient tree,
Whispers linger in the air.
Leaves murmur softly, free,
Echoes of a time laid bare.

Branches sway, a gentle dance,
Casting shadows on the ground.
Nature's song, a fleeting chance,
In the silence, hope is found.

Stories woven in each ring,
Time has carved its quiet tale.
Hear the memories they bring,
As the winds begin to wail.

Dreams are held within its heart,
Roots extend far and wide.
As the worlds around depart,
The echoing boughs abide.

In the twilight's muted glow,
Truth resides within the leaves.
Every gust a tale to know,
In the wood where time believes.

Chronicles of the Weathered Wood

Time has gnarled the weathered grain,
Each crevice holds a secret old.
Tales of joy, and echoes of pain,
In the silence, life's unfold.

Sunlight filters through the bark,
Casting patterns on the ground.
In its shadows, dreams can spark,
In each twist, a truth profound.

The forest speaks in softest tones,
To those who choose to take a pause.
Rustling leaves, like gentle moans,
In every sigh, nature's laws.

Carved by storms and gentle rain,
A history etched deep in sight.
Each knot a story, joy or strain,
In day's embrace, or starry night.

Around this wood, the world will spin,
Yet still it stands, so proud, so free.
Weathered wood holds memories thin,
In its silence, eternity.

Elegy for a Dying Grove

Once vibrant leaves kissed the skies,
Now they tremble, fade away.
Nature weeps, a soft goodbye,
As golden hues turn into gray.

Roots, once strong, now silently shake,
In the shadows, life retreats.
A mournful sigh, the branches break,
Where the heart of the forest beats.

Echoes of laughter blend with tears,
In the twilight's soft embrace.
Countless seasons mark the years,
Yet time has worn this sacred space.

Listen close to nature's plea,
In the rustling leaves' lament.
What was once a symphony,
Now a quiet, fading scent.

In solemn twilight, take your stand,
Let the whispers mark the loss.
For every grove that leaves the land,
We carry forth the heavy cross.

Echoes from Within

Nestled deep within the soul,
Whispers rise, a haunting song.
Echoes of a truth made whole,
In the stillness, we belong.

Chasing shadows, fears take flight,
Yet light breaks through the darkest veil.
In the heart, there's endless night,
But every echo tells the tale.

Memory dances on the breeze,
Flickers bright, then fades away.
Caught between the trees and leaves,
In longing whispers, here we stay.

Walls may close, but voices call,
From the depths, they will not cease.
In the silence, we stand tall,
Echoes weave our inner peace.

Together with the moonlit sky,
We rise and fall, a gentle wave.
For every echo that draws nigh,
Is a mark of love we crave.

Lullabies of the Night Wind

Whispers of dusk serenade the trees,
A gentle breeze cradles the night's ease.
Stars shimmer softly in the velvet sky,
While dreams take wing as the shadows sigh.

Moonlight dances on the silver stream,
Guiding lost souls through the weave of dreams.
In this silence, the world finds its song,
A lullaby sweet where we all belong.

Crickets play their symphony of night,
Nature's heartbeat pulses soft and light.
In the quiet, hopes begin to swell,
As the night wind weaves its soothing spell.

Rest now, dear heart, in this cradle of stars,
Let go of burdens, forget your scars.
For in this moment, peace calls your name,
Wrapped in the warmth of a lover's flame.

Close your eyes and let the dreams glide,
The night wind whispers; let love be your guide.
In the arms of the night, find solace and rest,
For in the lullabies, you're truly blessed.

Shade of the Sentinel

Under the watch of the ancient tree,
Whispers of history drift softly free.
Its branches extend like a guardian's arm,
Casting a shadow both sturdy and warm.

Leaves flutter softly in the warm breeze,
Carrying secrets of all that it sees.
Beneath its cover, the world seems to pause,
As nature unfolds its unspoken laws.

In the shade where the wildflowers grow,
Time feels suspended, slow like the flow.
Each petal a story, each stem a lost rhyme,
Blossoming softly beneath the old pine.

Children laugh under its patient watch,
In their playful hearts, they find love's match.
While the winds sing songs of forgotten days,
In the shade of the sentinel's gentle gaze.

Come sit a while, let the worries cease,
In the cool embrace, find your inner peace.
For here in the shade, love's roots intertwine,
Where the spirit wanders, forever divine.

Doorway to the Serene

Amidst the chaos, there lies a gate,
An entrance to calm, an end to fate.
Each step brings whispers of peace to the soul,
A heartfelt journey towards becoming whole.

The path is lined with blossoms in bloom,
Each petal unfolding dispelling the gloom.
Through the doorway, the burdens of time,
Fade into echoes of an old, distant chime.

The air is scented with lavender's grace,
A fragrant invitation to a tranquil space.
Softly it beckons, with arms open wide,
As the heart prepares to take its own stride.

Beyond the threshold, where still waters rest,
The spirit finds solace and quiet, its nest.
With each gentle wave that caresses the shore,
Comes the promise of peace, forevermore.

Step through the doorway, let worries unwind,
In the realm of the serene, true joy you'll find.
For here in the quiet, dreams tenderly gleam,
Awakening life in the heart's gentle dream.

Echoes of the Forgotten Path

Worn stones whisper of times long past,
Footsteps echo where memories last.
The path, though faded, invites the bold,
With tales of bravery yet to be told.

Gnarled roots twist and intertwine,
In the heart of the forest where shadows align.
Each bend in the trail uncovers a song,
The music of journeys, where we all belong.

Sunlight filters through leaves overhead,
Guiding the wanderers where few have tread.
With every step, the world starts to blend,
As nature and traveler, together, they mend.

Find solace in silence, let the stillness teach,
The echoes of paths that seem out of reach.
For in the forgotten, the heart shall discover,
The beauty of life from one journey to another.

So tread with honor where the wild winds sigh,
Listen to whispers of those who passed by.
In the echoes of the path, let your spirit rise,
For every footstep holds the nature of skies.

Roots of Longing

Deep in the earth, where shadows play,
Tangled roots reach, yearning to stay.
Whispers of love through soil they weave,
Holding the dreams that never leave.

Beneath the stars, beneath the night,
Longing echoes, a silent flight.
Branches above, they sway and sigh,
Searching the dark for a lighted sky.

In every heart, a gentle ache,
Promises made, but pathways break.
Fingers stretched to grasp the past,
While seasons change, and moments pass.

Rain falls softly, a tender balm,
In the storm, a hidden calm.
Roots entwined, they hold on tight,
Seeking solace in endless night.

Yet in this yearning, strength is found,
From longing's depths, we rise unbound.
With every tear, a seed is sown,
In the garden of our hearts, we've grown.

Leaves of Memory

Golden leaves drift in the breeze,
Whispers of time carried with ease.
Each one a tale, a moment spent,
In the tapestry of life, we're lent.

Colors fade as seasons change,
Memories shift, sometimes strange.
Yet in the rustle, stories stay,
Holding echoes of yesterday.

Through the winding paths we roam,
These leaves remind us of our home.
The laughter shared, the tears that fell,
Each leaf a story, a magic spell.

In autumn's glow, we find the light,
Chasing the past through day and night.
Leaves like pages turn and fall,
Whispering softly, we recall.

With every gust that sweeps the land,
Memories linger, brightly planned.
In nature's book, we pen our dreams,
A symphony of whispered themes.

Sanctuary of Silent Stories

In hushed corners where shadows dwell,
Silent stories yearn to tell.
Pages worn, they softly sigh,
Whispering secrets as time slips by.

Beneath the dust of forgotten days,
Echoes of laughter, a tender gaze.
In the quiet, the heart can hear,
Tales of joy, and tales of fear.

Sheltered here, beneath the guise,
Mysteries hide in gentle sighs.
Each word a comfort, a balmy embrace,
In this sanctuary, we find our place.

Flickering candles, a warm glow,
Where memories linger, timeless flow.
Through chapters read, we seek the truth,
Unveiling the wisdom of our youth.

In these still moments, the world stands still,
Stories unfold with grace and skill.
Sanctuary calls us to unwind,
In silent tales, our souls defined.

The Nestling's Lament

In a fragile nest, hope takes flight,
Small wings tremble in morning light.
Yet the sky looms vast and wide,
Fear tugs gently, a tender guide.

Whispers of winds beyond the rime,
Voices call across the clime.
In every flutter, doubts arise,
A nestling waits, beneath the skies.

With each soft chirp, a longing grown,
Yearning to soar, to find the unknown.
Yet safety's warmth, a soothing song,
Cradles the fears that feel so strong.

Past branches bent and skies of blue,
The nestling dreams of what is true.
In shadowed corners, hidden nests,
Whispers of courage through the quest.

One day the wings will learn to rise,
To dance with clouds, to touch the skies.
But till then, in comfort's thrall,
The nestling dreams, embracing all.

Enchanted Embrace

In the twilight glow, we dance,
Soft whispers fade, a fleeting chance.
Moonlight drapes its silver lace,
Wrapped in love, our warm embrace.

Stars above in silent gaze,
Shining bright through misty haze.
Hearts entwined in tender sighs,
Time stands still 'neath velvet skies.

Every moment feels so right,
Lost together, soul's delight.
In this realm where dreams take flight,
We linger on, through endless night.

Beyond the world, just you and me,
A secret place, our hearts decree.
In magic’s grasp, we find our way,
In enchanted night, forever stay.

With every breath, our spirits soar,
In this embrace, we seek for more.
Hand in hand, we'll explore the grace,
Of love that time cannot erase.

Where the Wild Things Whisper

In the forest, shadows play,
Wild things whisper, night and day.
Leaves that rustle, secrets share,
In hidden places, wild thoughts flare.

Moonlit paths where dreams convene,
Creatures dance, both shy and keen.
Echoes call from ancient trees,
Nature's pulse in every breeze.

Among the thickets, silence sighs,
A world alive with phantom cries.
Footsteps tread on fertile ground,
Lost in wonders, beauty found.

Beneath the stars, they spin and twirl,
In wild abandon, dreams unfurl.
Voices rise with the night air,
Where the wild things dance in bare.

Softly now, let worries cease,
In this magic, find your peace.
With wild heart, let spirits roam,
In whispered woods, discover home.

Guardian of the Lost Leaves

Amidst the trees, the guardian stands,
With weathered face and gentle hands.
Whispers carried on autumn's breath,
In fallen leaves, a tale of death.

Each rustling leaf, a memory's sigh,
Of days gone past, they flutter by.
In hues of gold, their stories weave,
The guardian stands, and none deceive.

Beneath the boughs, shadows play,
As twilight calls, the light fades away.
Silent promises in the dusk,
The calling woods, a fragrant musk.

Guarding dreams of those long lost,
Through changing seasons, through every frost.
The sacred trust in every tree,
In nature's heart, the echoes plea.

In whispered tones, the secrets hide,
With every leaf, the forest cried.
The guardian stands, a steadfast shield,
In twilight's glow, his fate revealed.

Beneath the Gnarled Limbs

Beneath the gnarled limbs, shadows creep,
In somber woods, where silence sleeps.
Echoes of laughter float on air,
In tangled roots, we find our prayer.

Branches twist, a web of fate,
In nature's grasp, we contemplate.
With every sigh, the world unwinds,
In sacred woods, our truth it finds.

A canopy of emerald dreams,
Where sunlight filters, softly gleams.
In every rustle, whispers call,
Beneath the limbs, we lose it all.

Time slips by in gentle flow,
In the heart of woods, we come to know.
The secrets hid in twilight's shade,
Beneath the limbs, our fears allayed.

Together here, we plant our roots,
In harmony, where nature hoots.
With every breath, we take our place,
Beneath the gnarled limbs, embraced in grace.

Dance of the Woodland Spirits

In twilight's gentle embrace, they sway,
Whispers of the leaves softly play.
Elfin laughter fills the air,
As shadows twirl without a care.

Mossy carpets underfoot gleam,
Flickering flames, a glistening dream.
Branches bow as they twine,
Nature's artists in design.

Glowing orbs like stars descend,
Guiding hearts that wish to blend.
With each step, a tale unfolds,
Of ancient secrets, rich and bold.

Light dances across the brook,
In hidden glades, the spirits look.
They spin and twist in harmony,
Echoes of their souls set free.

In this moment, magic lives,
An orchestra of nature gives.
With eyes closed, join the trance,
Embrace the woodland spirits' dance.

Chronicle of the Twisted Roots

Beneath the earth, a story lies,
Whispered softly, no need for guise.
Roots entwined in a tangled knot,
Silent secrets, all but forgot.

They reach for depth, they seek the past,
Anchored firm, their grip holds fast.
In shadows deep, where darkness dwells,
A chronicle of ancient spells.

Winds pull threads from times agone,
In each twist, a wisdom’s bone.
Gnarled fingers stretch to the sky,
Sipping rain and dreaming high.

Whispers echo in the breeze,
Nature's tales shake the trees.
Each root a story, every twist,
A memory lost in nature’s mist.

Together they weave the earth’s great quilt,
A saga of life, of love, of guilt.
In their embrace, the past resounds,
In silent woods, where time confounds.

Illuminated by Moonlight

Silver beams on waters gleam,
Casting whispers like a dream.
Under stars, the world lies still,
Lost in night's enchanting thrill.

Crickets sing their soft refrain,
While the night breathes through the grain.
A gentle pull, the tides will sway,
As nature hums, the shadows play.

The moon ascends, a glowing guide,
Leading lost souls, far and wide.
With soft caress, it lights the way,
Revealing secrets night can sway.

In the forest, a pathway glows,
Where only moonlit magic flows.
Stories drape on silhouettes,
A canvas of the night begets.

Embrace the calm, let spirits soar,
For through the night, there is much more.
In moonlit dreams, we deeply find,
A world of wonder, unconfined.

Where Time Stands Still

Amidst the mountains, ages fold,
Time's firm grasp, a story told.
In stillness deep, the echoes wane,
Moments linger, free from strain.

Whispers of the past entwine,
In quiet corners of the pine.
Time, a river flowing slow,
Where shadows dance, and breezes blow.

The sun and moon both share the space,
In harmony, they leave no trace.
A timeless realm where spirits dwell,
In this oasis, all is well.

Leaves rustle softly in the breeze,
Moments freeze among the trees.
Every heartbeat, every sigh,
In stillness, let the hours fly.

Here, the world can fade away,
In gentle peace, we choose to stay.
Where time stands still, our hearts can heal,
In nature's arms, we find what's real.

Veins of the Earth

Beneath the surface, life flows bright,
A network of roots in the dark of night.
Whispers of ages in silent streams,
Cradling the essence of ancient dreams.

Through crevices wide, the light seeps down,
Kissed by the soil, where secrets drown.
Nature's embrace in each tender trace,
The pulse of the planet, a constant grace.

Rivers of wisdom run deep below,
Carving the land with stories to show.
Time's gentle hand shapes rock and clay,
In the veins of the earth, life finds its way.

Mountains stand tall, guard the unseen,
Holding the breath of what might have been.
In silence, they listen to echoes of sound,
Veins of the earth, where truth can be found.

So tread softly on this sacred ground,
For in every corner, a mystery's found.
Breathe in the magic, let your spirit roam,
In the veins of the earth, always find home.

Rustling Dreams

In the twilight's hush, soft whispers flow,
Rustling dreams in the night's warm glow.
Stars sparkle gently, as if to say,
Let your heart wander, let worries lay.

Leaves dance lightly on a soft night breeze,
Carrying secrets through the slumbering trees.
Moonlight spills silver on paths yet untread,
Alluring the dreamers, guiding the led.

Night blooms with wishes, a delicate scent,
Every breath taken, a sweet lament.
Crickets serenade the closing day light,
With melodies weaving through the tapestry tight.

Time may be fleeting; our memories cling,
In the rustle of dreams, our spirits take wing.
Embraced by the night, we rise and we fall,
In this realm of wonder, we hear nature's call.

So lie on the grass, let thoughts drift away,
In the arms of the night, let your spirit sway.
For in rustling dreams, the world feels so bright,
Awakening hope in the stillness of night.

Cradle of Lost Voices

In the shadows of time, where echoes reside,
A cradle of lost voices, memories tied.
Whispers of laughter, soft cries of pain,
Drifting through ages like a gentle rain.

The stories of those who once walked the land,
Fading like footprints in soft, shifting sand.
Each tale a thread in the fabric of night,
A tapestry woven with dark and with light.

Haunted by moments that refuse to fade,
The songs of the ancients in silence conveyed.
From the valleys and hills, the past calls in vain,
A symphony woven from joy and from strain.

Listen closely, for the echoes remain,
In the heart's quiet chambers, love mingles with pain.
A cradle of voices that dance in the dark,
Linking the present, igniting a spark.

So cherish the stories that linger and fade,
For in every whisper, a memory's laid.
In the cradle of lost voices, we find our grace,
A reminder of time, in this sacred space.

Beneath the Gnarled Bark

Beneath the gnarled bark, secrets conspire,
Roots intertwine as if fueled by fire.
A haven for whispers, soft tales from the past,
Holding the dreams of a world unsurpassed.

In the stillness, where shadows dance bright,
Nature's embrace wraps the heart in delight.
Branches reach out, cradling the sky,
Drawing the stars with a soft lullaby.

Life teems in the crevices, thriving anew,
Each nook a story, a memory true.
Beneath every layer, a heartbeat resides,
In the gnarled bark's grip, a universe hides.

Moss blankets softly, a velvet cocoon,
Carrying whispers of the sun and the moon.
The dance of the seasons, the passage of time,
Beneath the gnarled bark, nature's own rhyme.

So wander the forest, let your spirit be free,
For beneath every surface, there's magic to see.
In the heartbeat of wood, in the rustle of leaves,
Beneath the gnarled bark, the soul believes.

Cradled in Nature's Silence

In the hush of dawn's embrace,
Whispers of the leaves interlace.
Gentle breezes calm the stream,
Nature's lullaby, a dream.

Mountains stand with quiet grace,
Sunlight paints their rugged face.
Birds take flight, their song so sweet,
Harmony in every beat.

Softly blooms the wildflower,
Dancing lightly, hour by hour.
Deer tread lightly on the ground,
In this peace, their hearts are found.

Stars emerge as day departs,
Filling skies with joyful arts.
Moonlight bathes the world in glow,
Cradled in night’s gentle flow.

Beneath the vast and endless dome,
Nature sings, we find our home.
In her silence, we are whole,
Cradled softly, heart and soul.

Mournful Roots in the Night

Underneath the weeping skies,
Silent cries and soft goodbyes.
Twisted branches, ancient sighs,
Echo tales of lost allies.

Moonlit shadows cast despair,
Whispers linger in the air.
Roots that grasp the ground so tight,
Mourn the warmth of fading light.

Echoes dance in hollow trees,
Carried softly by the breeze.
Memories of what once bloomed,
In the night, their silence loomed.

Stars above seem dimmed and pale,
Listening to the sorrowed tale.
Night unfolds its velvet shroud,
Where the mournful roots stand proud.

In the dark, the spirits wane,
Whispers filled with ghostly pain.
Yet in shadows, strength resides,
Mournful roots with hidden guides.

Seeds of Yesterday's Echo

In the soil where dreams are sown,
Tiny seeds of life are grown.
Whispers of the past remain,
Tales of joy, and echoes pain.

Time moves on, but echoes stay,
In the breeze, they find their way.
Stories hidden, waiting still,
In the heart, they whisper, will.

Sunset paints the sky in hues,
Of golden warmth and misty blues.
Every shadow, every light,
Holds the memory of the night.

Roots entangled, history's thread,
Planting dreams for those who've tread.
Seeds of hope beneath the earth,
Whispering of a new rebirth.

Through the seasons, life will flow,
From the past, our futures grow.
Echoes dance in every breeze,
Together bound, like ancient trees.

Tales from the Knotted Trunk

Under the branches, stories weave,
Ancient whispers, time's reprieve.
Each knot a chapter, aged and worn,
In the silent woods, legends are born.

Beneath the bark, secrets sleep,
Memories buried, their silence deep.
A wise old tree, holding its ground,
Echoes of laughter in leaves abound.

With every breeze, tales take flight,
Dancing shadows in the fading light.
A shelter for dreams, a guardian true,
The knotted trunk embraces you.

In summer's bloom or winter's chill,
Standing tall, it bends to will.
Roots entwined, spirits entwine,
Nature's heart, forever divine.

So linger awhile by the ancient wood,
Listen closely, you'll find it good.
For in the silence, stories too,
Whisper their secrets just for you.

Dreams in the Thicket

In the thicket where shadows play,
Dreams wander freely, night and day.
Cloaked in whispers, secrets are spun,
As dusk approaches, adventures begun.

Berries glisten under moon's gleam,
Nature weaves a soft, silken dream.
Rustling leaves share tales of woe,
And laughter of sprites, both high and low.

A pathway of light through tangled vines,
Guiding lost souls to hidden shrines.
A chorus of crickets, a soothing sound,
Where wonder and solace can always be found.

The thicket hums with delicate grace,
Inviting the dreamer to find their space.
In every nook where the wildflowers bloom,
The heart knows its home, dispelling the gloom.

So follow the echoes, let your spirit roam,
In the vibrant thicket, you're never alone.
For in every shadow where soft whispers sigh,
The essence of dreams will forever fly.

Reveries of the Hollow Shade

In the hollow shade, thoughts gently drift,
Time slows down, a precious gift.
Sunlight dapples on the cool ground,
Where hopes and dreams quietly abound.

A resting place beneath leafy boughs,
Inspired gazes, tranquil vows.
Through thick branches, the world feels new,
Cocooned in peace, just me and you.

With every sigh, the flowers sway,
In the hollow shade, we wish to stay.
Here stories linger, woven in air,
In the tender space, love lays bare.

The stillness hums with a gentle song,
As whispers of nature carry along.
A refuge where the heart can be free,
In the hollow shade, just you and me.

So come take a moment, breathe in the calm,
Let worries fade, let the spirit charm.
For in this cradle where shadows blend,
The hollow shade, our timeless friend.

Bygone Reveries

In the twilight of memory's haze,
Bygone reveries dance in a daze.
Fading echoes of laughter ring,
In the heart's quiet corners, they cling.

Time wears a veil, soft and thin,
In dreams of the past, we begin again.
Old photographs in sepia tones,
Whisper forgotten stories, like stones.

Each smile a moment, dear and bright,
Carved in the fabric of timeless light.
With every breath, nostalgia flows,
A garden of feelings, where memory grows.

And though seasons change, and time moves on,
Bygone reveries remain, never gone.
A tapestry woven of joy and pain,
They linger in shadows, like soft summer rain.

So cherish the past, let it unfold,
In the warmth of remembrance, hearts are bold.
For the tales of tomorrow are rooted in today,
Bygone reveries, our guiding ray.

Twilight Tales of the Verdant Realm

In the hush of twilight's glow,
Whispers dance where shadows grow.
Leaves of emerald softly sigh,
Secrets woven, low and high.

Mossy paths invite your feet,
Nature's rhythm, calm and sweet.
Silhouettes of ancient trees,
Guarding tales upon the breeze.

Stars awaken, one by one,
As the day is slowly done.
Crickets serenade the night,
Glowing fireflies, a gentle light.

Each turn carries a mournful tune,
Softened by the silver moon.
In the realm where wild things roam,
Every heart can find a home.

So linger long where stories thread,
In whispered woods where dreams are spread.
Embrace the twilight, hold it dear,
For in its peace, all things are clear.

Whispered Promises and Shattered Hope

In the shadows where hopes collide,
Whispers echo, hearts divided.
Promises like fleeting mist,
Slip away from clasping fist.

Beneath the weight of silence deep,
Lies the trust we couldn't keep.
Fragile dreams, now torn apart,
Fragments scattered, a wounded heart.

Through the haze of memories past,
Fleeting moments, never last.
Yet in the pain, a lesson told,
In every ending, new dreams unfold.

Time drifts softly, healing ways,
But shadows linger, in the blaze.
A candle flickers, hope reborn,
From shattered glass, new paths are worn.

So hold the whispers, let them flow,
Through the scars, allow them to grow.
In every ending lies a start,
From whispered promises in the heart.

Beneath the Weight of Time

Beneath the weight of endless sighs,
Time unfurls, a fleeting guise.
Hours slip through the cracks of days,
In silent pools where memory stays.

Each tick, a story yet untold,
In fleeting warmth, the young grow old.
Whispers drift like autumn leaves,
Carried by the breeze that grieves.

Captured moments, precious and rare,
In the stillness, memories stir the air.
Joy and sorrow intertwined,
Life's tapestry, carefully designed.

Yet amidst the shadows and light,
Hope blooms gently, within sight.
Each heartbeat, a promise anew,
Beneath the weight, strength comes through.

So gather time like flower seeds,
Plant them deep among the reeds.
In the garden of our minds,
The beauty of existence finds.

Secrets Among the Boughs

In the heart of the forest deep,
Secrets stir, and shadows creep.
Among the boughs where silence reigns,
Ancient whispers hide their chains.

Nestled roots and tangled vines,
Watchful eyes in the intertwines.
Every rustle, every sigh,
Tells a story, passing by.

Moonlight drips through leafy lace,
Illuminating a sacred space.
Here the whispers weave a spell,
Guarding the truths they cannot tell.

Friends of the night, they gather near,
Concealing hopes, revealing fear.
In this haven, tales are spun,
Among the boughs, all is one.

So listen close in twilight's song,
For the secrets have lingered long.
In nature's arms, they softly sway,
Guiding us along the way.

Solace Under the Green Canopy

Beneath the leaves, a gentle sigh,
Whispers dance as breezes fly.
Sunlight filters, warm and light,
A tranquil heart finds peace in sight.

Soft shadows play on forest floor,
Nature's song, a calming core.
Each rustle tells a story deep,
In leafy arms, the world can sleep.

Branches cradle wandering dreams,
Purling streams and silver beams.
Mossy beds, where silence reigns,
In echo's peace, the spirit gains.

The canopy of emerald hues,
Holds secrets shared with morning dews.
In this refuge, worries cease,
Nature’s embrace grants sweet release.

With every breath, the forest breathes,
A tapestry that gently weaves.
Here, solace blooms in every glance,
Under the green, our souls can dance.

Light and Shadow Entwined

Dancing light with shadows play,
In twilight's arms, they softly sway.
Golden rays in branches weave,
Secrets cast, and hearts believe.

Each moment caught, a fleeting glance,
Where day and night in silence dance.
Beneath the boughs, a world alive,
In gentle hues, dreams arrive.

Whispers to the stars above,
Echoes of a hidden love.
In shadows deep, we find our way,
Guided by the dusk and day.

Textures blend, a soft embrace,
In twilight's grip, we find our place.
Through light and dark, our spirits roam,
In every shadow, we call home.

As dusk descends and night awakes,
Magic stirs in every break.
Bathed in night's profound cocoon,
We dance beneath the watchful moon.

Tales of the Wind's Embrace

Whispers of the gentle breeze,
Carry tales through swaying trees.
Each leaf a story yet untold,
In every gust, a dream unfolds.

The sky adorned with clouds of cream,
Bears witness to the wind's sweet dream.
Across the hills, it sweeps and glides,
A woven path where hope abides.

With every sigh, the world can hear,
The laughter born from yesteryear.
In rustling grass, the echoes call,
The wind's embrace, it cradles all.

Through open fields, with arms so wide,
It beckons us to rise and glide.
To chase the whispers, bold and free,
In the wind’s story, we long to be.

So let us dance with every breeze,
Feel the stories, the memories tease.
In the gentle push and pull,
Tales of the wind, forever full.

In the Arms of Wood and Leaf

In the forest's warm embrace,
Wood and leaf find their own place.
Branches arching, roots entwine,
Nature's harmony, pure design.

Mossy carpets, soft and deep,
Where weary souls may gently sleep.
Whispers here, a sacred thread,
In wood and leaf, our fears are shed.

Carved by time, each tree stands tall,
Guardians against the world's sharp call.
Under canopies, love is sown,
In every rustle, we're not alone.

With every breath, the earth draws near,
In the arms of green, there’s no fear.
The forest speaks in tones of grace,
Inviting us to find our place.

So linger here, let spirits soar,
In wood and leaf, we ask for more.
Together, we will always thrive,
In this embrace, we feel alive.

www.ingramcontent.com/pod-product-compliance
Ingram Content Group UK Ltd.
Pitfield, Milton Keynes, MK11 3LW, UK
UKHW031957131224
452403UK00010B/498

9 789908 126067